PUPPIES and KITTENS 2

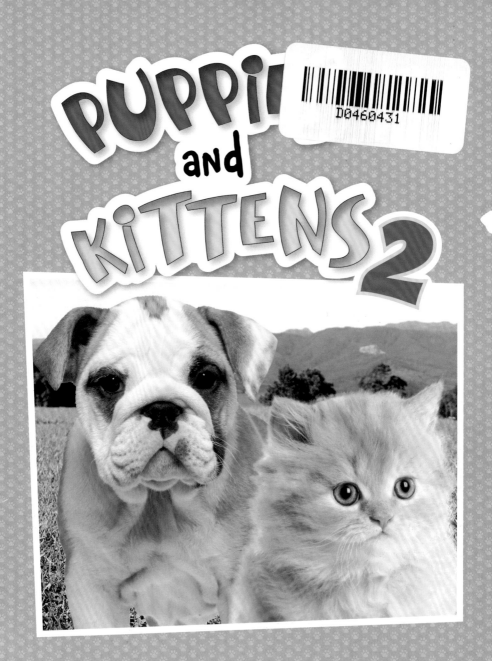

by Marilyn Easton

SCHOLASTIC INC.

There are about 78 million dogs living in houses all around the United States. This makes the U.S.A. the country with the most canine companions!

BOXER

In the United States, about 86 million cats are kept as pets. This makes cats the most popular pet in the U.S.A.

BiRMAN

The most popular dog in the United States is the Labrador retriever. This isn't breaking news—it's been this way for over 20 years!

LABRADOR RETRIEVER

The Persian is the most popular cat in the United States. This may be because owners love petting their beautiful, soft fur. This cat has held the top spot since 1871. That's before the airplane was invented!

For the first year of their lives, dogs are considered puppies. During this time, they learn how to play by interacting with their brothers and sisters.

For the first year of their lives, cats are considered to be kittens. Their moms keep them safe, warm, and well fed.

When it comes to height, the Great Dane is one of the tallest dogs. When most Great Danes stand on their back legs, they can be more than 6 feet tall. That's taller than some adult humans!

One of the largest domestic cats is called the Ragdoll. When they are adults, Ragdolls can weigh almost 30 pounds! That's more than double the weight of an average cat.

RAGDOLL

The dog with the longest, floppiest ears is the basset hound. Surprisingly, their large ears help them smell better by wafting scents toward their extra-sharp noses.

BASSET HOUND

The American Curl is known for its signature ears, which curl backward. They aren't born with this special look, though. Kittens are born with straight ears that curl when the kitten is about five days old.

AMERICAN CURL

The smallest dog is the Chihuahua. It can weigh from two to six pounds. These tiny dogs can fit inside a purse, so they are great for an owner who travels!

CHIHUAHUA

The Singapura is the smallest known domestic cat. They can weigh between four to six pounds. Because of their tiny size, adult cats are often confused with kittens!

SINGAPURA

When it comes to being loud, German shepherds are among the first to be heard. Their powerful bark helps alert their owners to danger. They also make excellent police dogs.

GERMAN SHEPHERD

The Siamese cat is considered the loudest and one of the most talkative cats. They're beautiful, but if you like peace and quiet, they may not be the best cat for you!

SIAMESE

One of the most popular hairless dogs is the Chinese crested. These dogs are often the winner of ugliest dog contests, although some people think they're so ugly that they're cute!

CHINESE CRESTED

The Sphynx is considered a hairless cat, but they are not totally hairless. They have a light fuzz that covers their skin. To keep warm, they love to cuddle up with their owners!

A poodle is a dog that usually loves water. In fact, in German, the name poodle means "puddle." The haircut they are known for was designed to help them swim more easily.

POODLE

Most cats run away at the sight of water. But the Turkish Van is known to enjoy a good swim! That may be because their special fur allows them to dry easily when they're done swimming.

TURKISH VAN

Golden retrievers love to play fetch! Their name comes from their strong desire to collect and return things, which is known as retrieving.

GOLDEN RETRIEVER

Retrieving isn't just for dogs. The Turkish Angora has been known to enjoy a good game of fetch.

Most dogs wag their tails to show they are happy, but the Pembroke Welsh corgi does not. This is because most corgis are born with a stumped, or bobbed, tail.

PEMBROKE WELSH CORGI

Some Manx cats have very short tails while others have no tails at all! The ones without tails are called rumpy. Most cats have 20 bones in their tails, but the rumpies' tails have between one and three bones.

The city of Boston is famous for many things, including the Boston terrier. That's right, this dog breed was first born in Boston right about the time when the Civil War ended.

BOSTON TERRIER

Cats come from all over the world, but the Maine coon is the only one that can trace its beginnings to the United States.

MAINE COON

Most people believe a dog's mouth is cleaner than a human's, but this is simply not true—especially if you really think about where a dog's mouth has been! A dog's mouth has some bacteria that will not affect humans, but overall their mouths are dirtier.

DACHSHUND

A cat's tongue can feel rough.
That's because of tiny hooks,
called papillae, on its tongue.
The papillae are designed
to help cats hold items
in their mouths.

SCOTTISH FOLD

A dog's whiskers are similar to a human's fingers. They can tell the dog certain things about his surroundings. Some whiskers are near the nose, while others are above the eyes. The whiskers above the eyes help prevent dust from getting inside.

Cat whiskers help cats experience the world around them. They use their whiskers to measure tight spaces to see if they can squeeze inside.

Border collies are very curious animals. A dog named Laika was even more curious, though. She was the first living mammal to travel to outer space. That's one small step for dog, one giant leap for animals everywhere!

BORDER COLLIE

Norwegian Forest cat owners
think their kitties are pretty
special, but there is one cat
who is out of this world.
In the fall of 1963, a cat named
Félicette was the first cat
to venture into space.

If you see a Maltese that is brown or gray, it is actually not a Maltese. It is likely a mixed breed. Maltese only come in one color—white!

MALTESE

It doesn't matter if you love dogs or cats, one thing is for sure—puppies and kittens are totally cute!